GOSPEL ESSENTIALS

Why the Bible's Message about Jesus Christ Is Good News!

Written by Dr. Daniel R. Carfrey

Xulon PRESS

GOSPEL ESSENTIALS
by Dr. Daniel R. Carfrey

Printed in the United States of America

ISBN 9781619969735

www.xulonpress.com

ACKNOWLEDGEMENTS

In my first book, *The Mysterious Disappearance*, published by Xulon Press in 2008, I made reference to some key persons in my life who greatly influenced me in my service for the Lord. On this occasion, I would like to thank all Christian leaders and churches who have been faithful to proclaim the Good News about the Lord Jesus Christ. My personal involvement has been with those of the Independent Baptist and Independent Bible Church movements. I called upon Jesus to be my personal Lord and Savior at the young age of six. I am now sixty years older. Jesus means more to me now than ever.

I have not seen Him with my physical eyes, but He lives within my heart. As the apostle Peter wrote to those in his day who had never personally seen the Lord, *"Whom having not seen, ye love; in whom, though now ye see him not, yet believing, ye rejoice with joy unspeakable and full of glory, (Peter 1:8).* It is with that same love for Him that I have undertaken to write this book. My hope is that, if you do not know Jesus Christ as your personal Lord and Savior, what is written in these pages will help you come to that knowledge by personal experience.

TABLE OF CONTENTS

Prelude . . . . **ix**

Answers to key questions about which the Gospel

of Jesus Christ is Good News!

Chapter One: What about who Jesus Is? 11

Chapter Two: What about Jesus' Birth? 20

Chapter Three: What about Jesus' Life

                             and Ministry? 28

Chapter Four: What about Jesus' Death? 39

Chapter Five: What about Jesus' Resurrection? . . . 52

Chapter Six: What about Jesus' Ascension

                             into Heaven? 60

Chapter Seven: What about Jesus' Coming Again? . . . 66

Chapter Eight: What about Your Response? 77

Conclusion **87**

PREFACE

I n the previous *Acknowledgements* I mentioned that I called upon the Lord Jesus Christ to be my personal Savior at the age of six. I didn't know much at that age, but I do know Jesus saved me. Over the sixty years since that day, I have been learning about what God did to provide salvation for me through the person of the Lord Jesus Christ. This includes being raised in a Christian home of a pastor who believed in the truth of the Bible from cover to cover; this includes being brought up in local churches that also believed in the truth of God's Word; this includes five years at a fundamental, Bible-believing Christian college; this includes four years of special training for the ministry at a Bible-believing theological seminary; and this includes over thirty years of ministry in planting Bible-believing churches and teaching future preachers of the Gospel at a Bible-believing college.

Did you notice how often I used the adjective "Bible-believing?" That is the purpose of this book. My purpose is to explain from the message of the Bible the Good News about Jesus Christ. I do not enter into arguments with people who do not believe the Bible. I simply ask them to give the Bible a fair hearing, and God will prove His own Word to their hearts.

My challenge to readers who cannot say that Jesus Christ is their personal Savior, is to attempt to read this entire book in one sitting. Am I talking to you, dear reader? If you do this, I believe you will respond to Jesus Christ as God commands in order for you to receive God's promise of eternal life. If you do know that Jesus Christ is your personal Savior, I encourage you to also read through every chapter. A review of these basic truths will thrill your heart and renew your enthusiasm to share the Good News about Jesus to everyone who will listen. Furthermore, I believe that there will be some information that will challenge you in your own understanding of the message of Jesus Christ, even if you have been a Christian for a number of years.

I was asked a question as I was writing this book, whether this would be a book for the average person to read, or a book oriented more towards the academic community. My answer was that this would be a book for the common person to read. It is for that reason that I have not included quotations from outside sources. The quotations I include will all be from the most authoritative source to back up the claims of Christianity about Jesus Christ: the Bible itself. There will be plenty of references to what God has to say in the Holy Scriptures, both the Old and New Testaments.

The Biblical quotations will all be set apart with the same kind of italic script, and the key words and phrases of the verses being quoted that support the point being made will be underlined. I realize that many today are not as familiar with the beloved King James Translation of the Bible. So I have included in the quotations some comments of my own in brackets [ ], in order to clarify what the verse is saying or is intended to say in my opinion.

The format I will follow will be simple. In each chapter, I summarize various essential truths involved in the Gospel of Jesus Christ. Just as key ingredients are specified for preparing a particular food, without which the meal being prepared would lack in taste and in quality; in the same way what is included in this book are key ingredients of the Christian Faith, without which the Gospel message about Jesus Christ would not be Good News.

CHAPTER ONE
WHAT ABOUT WHO JESUS IS?

✝

Introduction

The Bible is not one book. It is a collection of sixty-six books written over a period of hundreds of years, in which the God of the Bible revealed His plan to provide a Savior for all. This is very important to know; for if the Bible is true, then the belief of Christians that Jesus Christ of Nazareth is the only true Savior is based on historical evidence.

While Jesus is described by many different names in the Bible, there are three that summarize who Christians believe him to be. Those three were stated by the apostle Paul to the Roman jailor, when he said for him to *"Believe on the <u>Lord Jesus Christ</u>, and thou shalt be saved..., (Acts 16:31)."*

Lord

The Meaning of the Name "Lord"

The English word "lord" is used to translate the Greek word *kurios* in the New Testament. It basically means "master" or "ruler." <u>The explanations of any Greek or Hebrew word in this book are based upon information that can be verified by consulting any Greek Lexicon.</u> When referring to humans, this Greek word is usually a title given to someone in authority.

> *Even as Sara obeyed Abraham, <u>calling him</u>*
> <u>*lord*</u> **[or head of her home]** . . . *1 Peter 3:6*

When the word is used in the New Testament to refer to Jesus Christ, the term refers to the common use in that day to one's belief in a <u>deity</u>, or a ruler worshipped as being a god.

> *...we know that an idol is nothing in the world, and that there is none other God but one. For though there be that are called gods, whether in heaven or in earth, (as <u>there be gods many</u>, and <u>lords many</u>,) But to us there is but <u>one God</u>, the Father, of whom are all things, and we in him; and <u>one Lord Jesus Christ</u>, by whom are all things, and we by him. 1 Corinthians 8:4-6*

Paul is saying that while the world of his day revered many deities they called "gods" and "lords," Christians only believe in using those terms to refer to God the Father and His divine Son, the Lord Jesus Christ. The Bible speaks of God as being one in divine essence, but eternally existing as three separate persons. It is in the name of this one Triune God that all of Christ's disciples are to be baptized.

> *Go ye therefore, and teach all nations, baptizing them in the <u>name of the Father</u>, and <u>of the Son</u>* [the Lord Jesus Christ], *and <u>of the Holy Ghost</u>* [or Holy Spirit]. *Matthew 28:19*

If Jesus is not God, then he was not a good man, nor a good teacher, nor a good prophet. He would have been one of the greatest imposters of all time. For Jesus claimed to be the divine Son of God sent forth to this earth from his Father in heaven, and it is for that reason that some tried to stone him for blasphemy.

> *Therefore the Jews sought the more to kill him, because he not only had broken the Sabbath, but <u>said also that God was his Father, making himself equal with God</u>.*

Jesus accepted the worship of his disciples.

> *And Thomas answered and said unto him* [Jesus], *<u>My Lord and my God</u>. Jesus saith unto him, Thomas, because thou hast seen me, thou hast believed: <u>blessed are they that have not seen, and yet have believed</u>. John 20:28-29*

In fact, the apostle John went on to declare that one's eternal destiny would depend upon their willingness to worship Jesus.

> *But these are written, that ye might believe that Jesus is the Christ, the <u>Son of God</u>; and that believing <u>ye might have life though his name</u>. John 20:31*

The Significance of the Name "Lord"

The significance of the name "Lord" in the Bible, as it pertains to Jesus Christ of Nazareth, is that Jesus is the only human whom Christians worship as their God. It also signifies that when Jesus was born as a baby in a manger, that this was not his beginning; for he had always existed from eternity as God with no beginning and with no end.

> *In the beginning* [of all creation] *was the Word* [referring to Jesus Christ], *and the Word was with*

13

God [the Father], *and the Word was God. John 1:1*

And the Word <u>was made flesh</u> [or became a man] *and dwelt among us, (and <u>we beheld his glory</u>, the <u>glory as of the only begotten of the Father</u>,) full of grace and truth. John 1:14*

Jesus Christ the same <u>yesterday, and today, and forever</u>. Hebrews 13:8

The fact that Jesus Christ of Nazareth is the eternal God is why God the Father commanded all of His angels to worship the baby Jesus when he was born.

And again, <u>when</u> he [God the Father] *<u>bringeth in the firstbegotten</u>* [or His firstborn divine Son, Jesus Christ] *<u>into the world</u>, he saith, And let <u>all the angels of God</u> <u>worship him</u>. Hebrews 1:6*

It is His birth as a human that leads us to discuss his name as also being "Jesus."

<u>Jesus</u>

<u>The Meaning of the Name "Jesus"</u>

The name *Jesus* in the Greek language is the same as the Hebrew name for *Joshua*. Its root meaning is that the "Lord" or "Jehovah" saves! This was the name that the angel of God commanded Joseph to give to the Christ child that would be born of the virgin Mary. The salvation that Jesus would bring to mankind would be deliverance from the penalty of sin.

And she [the Virgin Mary] *shall bring forth a son, and thou* [Joseph] *shalt call his name*

*JESUS: for he shall <u>save</u> his people <u>from their</u>
<u>sins</u>. Matthew 1:21*

Joseph was betrothed to Mary when the angel spoke
these words to him. Under Jewish law they were officially
man and wife, even though they had not yet come to live
together as a man and wife.

> *Then Joseph being raised from sleep did as the*
> *angel of the Lord had bidden him, and took unto*
> *him his wife* [Mary]: *And knew her not* [in an
> intimate way as his wife] *till she had brought*
> *forth her firstborn son: and he* [Joseph] *called*
> *his name JESUS. Matthew 1:24-25*

<u>The Significance of the Name "Jesus"</u>

Had Jesus not become a man, we would have no Savior!
He became a man for three reasons: <u>First</u>, God is spirit, eternal in nature, and cannot die. So the Son of God became a
man in order to die in our place and pay the penalty of our
sins. <u>Second</u>, the price that Jesus would pay with his own
blood would be valuable enough in the sight of the Father to
justify forgiving those who believe in his name from any and
all of their sins forever.

> *Forasmuch as ye know that ye were not <u>redeemed</u>*
> [or set free from the penalty of your sins] *with*
> *corruptible things, as silver and gold,...But <u>with</u>*
> <u>*the precious blood of Christ*</u>*,...Who verily was*
> *foreordained* [or planned ahead of time by God
> the Father] *before the foundation of the world* [or
> before this world was created], *but was manifest*
> [or brought into the world] *in these last times for*
> *you. 1 Peter 1:18-20*

And <u>third</u>, the fact that God would send His only begotten Son into the world to die for our sins would demonstrate just how much the Father loves us and wants to save us.

> <u>*For God so loved the world, that he gave his only*</u>
> <u>*begotten Son,*</u> *that whosoever believeth in him*
> *should not perish, but have everlasting life. John*
> *3:16*

It is important to note that Jesus died for the sins of all mankind of his own free will. He volunteered to lay down his life, and was loved by his Father for doing so.

> *Therefore* <u>*doth my Father love me,*</u> <u>*because I lay*</u>
> <u>*down my life*</u>*, that I might take it again. No man*
> *taketh it from me, but* <u>*I lay it down of myself.*</u> <u>*I*</u>
> <u>*have power to lay*</u> *it* <u>*down*</u>*, and I have power to*
> *take it again . . . John 10:17-18*

So God's eternal divine Son became a man in order to die in our place for our sins. The name Jesus pertains to his <u>first coming</u> into this world to be our Savior. This leads us to the third special name that describes his person.

Christ

The Meaning of the Name "Christ"

The name "Christ" is derived from the Greek name *Christos*, and is the name the Jews chose to use for the Hebrew term *Messiah*. The name means "The Anointed One" and refers to God's future divine King whom God promised would come to this world in order to establish God's kingdom on earth. It was God's pattern to install of His divinely appointed leaders with the anointing or pouring of oil upon the head.

The promise that Jesus will one day return to this earth to rule as God's divine King is the good news or "gospel of the kingdom" that was preached by Christ's apostles and prophets.

> *And Paul dwelt two whole years in his own hired house, and received all that came in unto him, preaching the kingdom of God, and teaching those things which concern the Lord Jesus Christ, with all confidence, no man forbidding him. Acts 28:30-31*

The Significance of the Name "Christ"

Christ's return to institute God's kingdom upon this present earth is the time period Jesus told his disciples to pray for.

> *After this manner therefore pray ye: Our Father which art in heaven, Hallowed be thy name. Thy kingdom come. Thy will be done in earth, as it is in heaven. Matthew 6:9-10*

This is the time period Christ's disciples were hoping to see fulfilled in their lifetime.

> *When they therefore were come together, they asked of him, saying, Lord, wilt thou <u>at this time restore again the kingdom</u> to Israel? Acts 1:6*

It is this second coming of Jesus to this earth that Christians look forward to.

> *Confirming the souls of the disciples, and exhorting them to continue in the faith, and that we must through much tribulation* [or suffering now] <u>*enter into the kingdom of God*</u>. *Acts 14:22*

<u>In Summary</u>

The name "Lord Jesus Christ" sums up what Christians believe about Jesus of Nazareth. They believe him to be their Lord and eternal God. They believe that he became a man in order to die for the sins of all mankind. And they believe that he is coming again as God's King in order to crush God's enemies and establish God's kingdom upon this earth. The following chart will help one to visualize these truths concerning Jesus' names.

Illustrative Chart of the Name, Lord Jesus Christ

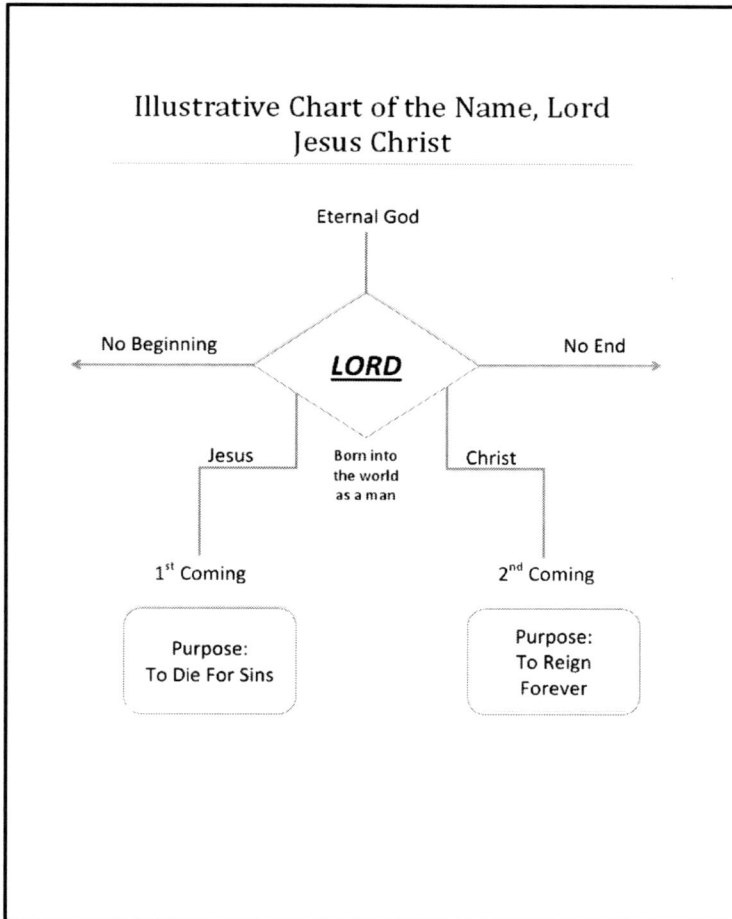

Illustrative Chart of the Name, Lord
Jesus Christ

Eternal God

No Beginning

LORD

No End

Jesus

Born into
the world
as a man

Christ

1ˢᵗ Coming

2ⁿᵈ Coming

Purpose:
To Die For Sins

Purpose:
To Reign
Forever

CHAPTER TWO
WHAT ABOUT JESUS' BIRTH?

Introduction

Hundreds of years before Jesus was born, God the Father had foretold in the Old Testament how to identify the promised Savior. We will examine <u>God's promise made to Abraham and to King David</u>, and <u>then show how Jesus Christ of Nazareth is the only man born in the world who fully met those qualifications in the Virgin Birth</u>.

God's Promise to Abraham

Abram or Abraham lived around two thousand years before Jesus was born. God told him to leave his country near the Persian Gulf and go to a land He promised to give to him. This land turned out later to be the land of Israel. Because he worshipped the only true God and creator of us all, God promised to not only bless him personally, but to bless all the nations of the world through him.

> *Now the Lord had said unto Abram, Get thee out of thy country, and from thy kindred, and from thy father's house* [who was an idolater], *unto a land that I will shew thee. And I will make of thee a great nation* [Jewish nation of Israel], *and I will bless thee, and make thy name great; and thou*

shalt be a blessing: And I will bless them that bless thee, and curse him that curseth thee: and in thee shall all families of the earth be blessed.
Genesis 12:1-3

God later clarified that it would be through one person descended from Abraham's son Isaac through whom God would bless all nations. He made this promise after Abraham was willing to sacrifice his son Isaac on one of the mountains of Moriah in obedience to God's command. God never intended for Abraham to actually kill his son, but Abraham didn't know that. God stopped Abraham from using his knife, and gave him the following promise:

And the angel of the Lord called unto Abraham out of heaven the second time, And said, By myself have I sworn, saith the Lord, for because thou hast done this thing, and hast not withheld thy son, thine only son: That in blessing I [God] *will bless thee, and in multiplying I will multiply thy seed* [Isaac] *as the stars of the heaven, and as the sand which is upon the sea shore* [the nation of Israel descended from Abraham and Isaac]*; and thy seed shall possess the gate of his enemies;And in thy seed* [singular] *shall all the nations of the earth be blessed; because thou hast obeyed my voice. Genesis 22:15-18*

Notice that God did not promise to bless all nations through the multiplied seeds that descended from Abraham, but through only one seed or offspring, which is Christ. The apostle Paul made reference to this promise in his epistle to the Galatians.

Now to Abraham and his seed were the promises made. He [God] saith not, And to seeds, as of many; but as of one, And to thy seed, which is Christ. Galatians 3:16

There were three reasons God commanded Abraham to sacrifice his only son. The first reason was to portray another Father/Son sacrifice that would take place many years later on those same mountains of Moriah. Only this time, God the Father would not spare His only Son Jesus, but would allow him to be sacrificed on another altar of sacrifice for our sins, that being the cross.

He that spared not his own Son, but delivered him up for us all, how shall he not with him also freely give us all things? Romans 8:32

Abraham was able to later understand that God intended for His command to portray the death of Jesus Christ on the cross many years later, and named the mountain where this took place to signify that future event.

And Abraham called the name of that place Jehovah-jireh: as it is said to this day, In the mount of the Lord it shall be seen. Genesis 22:14

A second reason was for God to set Himself apart from the pagan gods being worshipped by those living in the land where Abraham lived. Pagan worshippers did sacrifice their sons to their gods, whereas God made it clear in the moral Law He later gave to Moses that such a practice was an abomination in His sight.

. . . for every abomination to the Lord, which he hateth, have they done unto their gods; for even

their sons and their daughters they have burnt in
the fire to their gods. Deuteronomy 12:31

The <u>third</u> reason was to test Abraham's faith in the Lord, whereby God could reward him with a blessing.

By faith Abraham, when he was tried, offered
up Isaac: and he that had received the promis-
es offered up his only begotten son, Of whom it
is said, That in Isaac shall thy seed be called:
Accounting that God was able to raise him up,
whence also he received him in a figure. Hebrews
11:17-19

For when God made promise to Abraham,
because he could swear [or pronounce an oath]
by no greater, he sware by himself, Saying, Surely
blessing I will bless thee, and multiplying I will
multiply thee. And so, after he had patiently
endured, he obtained the promise. Hebrews
6:13-15

God's Promise to King David

David was the second king of the nation Israel. He was a man after God's own heart because he usually obeyed God. And in the most notorious case when he didn't, he fully and genuinely repented of his sin and did not resent God's discipline that came upon him for his sin. Since he was so different in attitude towards God than Saul, the first king of Israel, God promised that the future Christ or God's Anointed King would come forth from David's loins.

And when thy days be fulfilled, and thou shalt
sleep with thy fathers, I will set up thy seed [or

offspring] *after thee, which shall proceed out of thy bowels, and I will establish his kingdom...* <u>*And thine house and thy kingdom shall be established forever before thee: thy throne shall be established forever.*</u> *2 Samuel 7:12,16*

God later revealed to King David that this son would be the Christ, and that he would be the divine Son of God as well as David's son. This information was given to David a thousand years before Jesus Christ was born. As he wrote in one of his psalms:

Why do the heathen [or nations] *rage, and the people imagine a vain thing? The kings of the earth set themselves, and the rulers take counsel together, against the Lord* [God the Father], *and <u>against his anointed</u>* [or the Christ], *saying, Let us break their bands asunder, and cast away their cords from us. He that sitteth in the heavens* [God the Father] *shall laugh: the Lord shall have them in derision. Then shall he speak unto them in his wrath, and vex them in his sore displeasure. Yet have I set my king* [the coming Christ] *upon my holy hill of Zion* [Jerusalem]. *I will declare the decree: the Lord* [God the Father] *hath said unto me* [the coming king or Christ], <u>*Thou art my Son; this day have I begotten thee*</u>. *Psalm 2:1-7*

The Virgin Birth of Jesus Christ of Nazareth

The fact that Jesus Christ was born of Mary fulfills God's promise that the Savior would be born a Jew, descended from the loins of Abraham and Isaac. The fact that Jesus was born of Mary also fulfills God's promise that the Savior would be born in the loins of king David as the promised Messiah or Christ.

Matthew begins his Gospel account with proof that Jesus is the one God promised, for he begins with the opening statement that Jesus Christ was born of both Abraham and David.

The book of the generation of Jesus Christ, the son of David, the son of Abraham. Matthew 1:1

The fact that Jesus was born of Mary when she was yet a virgin fulfills the promise that Jesus is God's divine Son.

> *And the angel said unto her, Fear not, Mary: for thou hast found favour with God. And, behold, thou shalt conceive in thy womb, and bring forth a son, and shalt call his name JESUS. He shall be great, and <u>shall be called the Son of the Highest</u> [God the Father]: and the Lord God shall give unto him <u>the throne of his father David</u>: And he shall <u>reign over the house of Jacob</u> [or Israel] <u>forever; and of his kingdom there shall be no end</u>.*

It should also be noted that since Jesus had no human father, He was not born with the sin nature that has been passed down through Adam. As the apostle Paul wrote, "Wherefore, as by one man sin entered into the world, and death by sin . . ." Romans 5:12. Jesus was born as the "holy one of God."

> *Then said Mary unto the angel, <u>How shall this be, seeing I know not a man</u> [intimately]? And the angel answered and said unto her, The Holy Ghost [or Holy Spirit] shall come upon thee, and the power of the Highest [or God the Father] shall overshadow thee: therefore also that <u>holy thing</u> [or One] <u>which shall be born of thee shall be called the Son of God</u>. Luke 1:30-35*

In Summary

Jesus Christ of Nazareth is the only person whose roots match the description given by the God of the Bible as to the promised Savior of the world. Christianity is a religion in that believers have guidelines to follow in obedience to Christ. But Christianity is more than a religion. It is a personal relationship with God through faith in the Lord Jesus Christ. As the apostle John wrote referring to Jesus, "He that hath the Son hath life; and he that hath not the Son of God hath not life," 1 John 5:12. It is as simple as that.

Illustrative Chart of Jesus' Human Genealogy

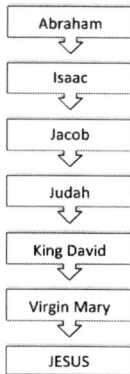

Illustrative Chart of Jesus' Human
Genealogy

Abraham

Isaac

Jacob

Judah

King David

Virgin Mary

JESUS

Son of Abraham, Son of David, Son of God

CHAPTER THREE
WHAT ABOUT JESUS' LIFE AND MINISTRY?

Introduction

Not only do Christians point to Jesus of Nazareth as being the only person born among men who met the qualifications in his birth to be the Savior of the world, but they also point to the testimony of those who were eye witnesses of his life and ministry. No one lived the kind of life Jesus did. No one had the kind of ministry that Jesus had. We will look at the <u>significance of his life in growing up to manhood</u>, the <u>significance of his miracles</u>, the <u>significance of the message</u> he proclaimed, and the <u>significance of his sinlessness</u> in order to be our Savior.

The Significance of Jesus' Life Growing Up

The prophets had foretold that the coming Christ God would send into the world to save mankind from their sins, would be recognized by his unique birth and by the kind of life he would live growing up. He would be the only person who, from the time of his conception in his mother's womb to the time of his death, would live in perfect obedience to God the Father who sent Him. As such, when he died on the cross, it would be for our sins, not his own.

The prophets, in foretelling the death of the coming Messiah, spoke of his knowing God from his mother's womb. He knew who his heavenly Father was, and He knew who sent him into the world to die for our sins.

> *I* [the coming Christ] *was cast upon thee* [God] *from the womb: thou art my God from my moth-er's belly. Psalm 22:10*

Jesus pointed out to Joseph and Mary who his Father was (when he was twelve years old), and it wasn't Joseph.

> *And he* [Jesus] *said unto them* [Mary and Joseph], *How is it that ye sought me? Wist ye not that I must be about my Father's business? Luke 2:49*

Even though Joseph was not his human father, Jesus nevertheless showed respect for him and his mother while being raised by them during his childhood. The New Testament claims that the community at large knew that God was with him in a special way.

> *And the child grew, and waxed strong in spirit, filled with wisdom: and the grace of God was upon him. Luke 2:40*

> *And Jesus increased in wisdom and stature, and in favour with God and man. Luke 2:52*

The Significance of Jesus' Miracles

Scholars differ on the length of time Jesus ministered on earth, but all agree that it was no more than three years. Jesus came to the nation of Israel because God had promised to bless all nations through the offspring of Abraham and Isaac.

But God would not bless the nation Israel and then extend that blessing to all the nations of the earth, unless Israel repented of their sins and accepted His divine Son as the Christ.

In order to prove to Israel that he was the divine Son of God, Jesus performed a number of miracles, both in quantity and in quality, which no other person on earth has performed. The following is a brief summary of some of the miracles Jesus performed:

Jesus turns water into wine. John 2:1-11
Jesus performs miracles at the Temple in Jerusalem. John 2:23-25
Jesus heals a nobleman's son from a distance away, who was near death. John 4:46-54
Jesus heals a demon possessed man in Capernaum. Luke 4:31-37
Jesus heals Peter's mother-in-law of a bed-ridden fever. Luke 4:38-39
Jesus heals multitudes of many diseases at Peter's home. Luke 4:40-41
Jesus heals all kinds of sickness and disease throughout Galilee. Luke 4:44
Jesus enables His disciples to catch a multitude of fish in the Sea of Galilee. Luke 5:6-10
Jesus heals a man of his leprosy. Luke 5:12-16
Jesus' fame spreads to the point He can no longer enter a city publicly. Mark 1:40-45
Jesus heals a paralyzed man. Luke 5:17-26
Jesus heals a man with a withered hand. Luke 6:6-11
Crowds press just to touch Jesus for His healing. Mark 3:7-10
Jesus enables his twelve disciples to heal. Mark 3:13-19
Jesus heals multitudes again around the Sea of Galilee. Luke 6:17-19
Jesus heals the servant of a Roman centurion by His

word alone. Luke 7:1-10

Jesus raises a widow's son from the dead. Luke 7:11-17

Jesus calms the wind and the sea during a storm on the Sea of Galilee. Luke 8:23-25

Jesus casts a multitude of demons out of a man into a herd of swine. Luke 8:26-33

Jesus heals a woman who has a blood disease when she touches Him. Luke 8:43-48

Jesus raises a ruler of the synagogue's daughter from the dead. Luke 8:49-56

Jesus heals two blind men. Matthew 9:27-31

Jesus heals a demon possessed man who was both blind and mute. Matthew 9:32-34

Jesus sends forth His twelve disciples again with power to heal. Luke 9:1-6

Jesus heals a man who had been paralyzed thirty-eight years. John 5:2-9

Jesus feeds more than 5000 with five loaves and two fish. John 6:2-13

Jesus walks on water to his disciples in the Sea of Galilee. John 6:16-21

Jesus casts a demon out of a daughter in Tyre and Sidon. Mark 7:24-30

Jesus heals a great multitude of various illness and diseases. Matthew 15:29-31

Jesus heals a man who is both deaf and mute. Mark 7:31-37

Jesus feeds 4000 with seven loaves and a few small fish. Mark 8:1-9

Jesus heals a blind man near Bethsaida. Mark 8:22-26

Jesus causes his face to shine like the sun. Matthew 17:1-8

Jesus heals a son who has epilepsy. Matthew 17:14-21

Jesus causes Peter to catch a fish with a coin in its mouth. Matthew 17:24-27

Jesus heals a man in Jerusalem who was blind from birth. John 9:1-7

Jesus gives seventy men power to heal in his name. Luke 10:1-24

Jesus casts a demon out of a man who is mute. Luke 11:14

Jesus heals ten lepers on his journey to Jerusalem. Luke 17:11-14

Jesus raises Lazarus after he had been dead four days. John 11:38-44

Jesus heals a blind man near Jericho. Luke 18:35-43

Jesus heals blind Bartimaeus on the way out of Jericho. Mark 10:46-52

Jesus heals two other blind men on the way out of Jericho. Matthew 20:29-34

Jesus causes a fig tree to wither. Mark 11:12-26

While an account of most of these miracles were recorded in two or more of the four Gospels (Matthew, Mark, Luke, and John), only one account is listed above for the sake of convenience. The apostle John wrote in the conclusion of his Gospel account that much more could be written about the ministry Jesus had on earth, but that there would not be enough books written to cover all that he and his fellow disciples saw and heard Jesus do and say.

> *And there are also many other things which Jesus did, the which, if they should be written every one, I suppose that even the world itself could not contain the books that should be written. Amen. John 21:25*

The Significance of Jesus' Message

The miracles that Jesus performed was to convince those who saw him that he was indeed the one God the Father had always promised to send into the world. Peter said as much in his proclamation to the first Gentile converts.

> *The word which God sent unto the children of Israel, preaching peace by Jesus Christ: (he is Lord of all:) That word, I say, ye know, which was published throughout all Judea, and began from Galilee, after the baptism which John preached: How God anointed Jesus of Nazareth with the Holy Ghost and with power: who went about doing good, and healing all that were oppressed of the devil; for God was with him. Acts 10:36-38*

Just as Jesus did the will of his Father as confirmed by the multitude of miracles which he did, Jesus also came to fulfill the message his Father sent him to proclaim. The Jews of that day wanted the Christ to come and deliver them from the Roman Empire. They were not interested in Christ's demand that they repent of their sins against the Law of God. Jesus warned them, in his famous Sermon on the Mount, to not think that he had come to give them the promised kingdom without first calling them to repent of their sins against the moral Law of his heavenly Father who had sent him.

> *Think not that I am come to destroy the law, or the prophets: I am not come to destroy, but to fulfill. Matthew 5:17*

That is the last thing the nation of Israel wanted to hear. They wanted the blessing of God, but they didn't want to hear about the moral law of God and their need to repent of their sins. Jesus rebuked them for following him simply because of what he could do in helping them to meet their daily needs. He told them they needed to be learning, as a result of seeing his miracles, of their need to listen to what he had to say on behalf of his Father who had sent him to provide eternal life for them.

> *Jesus answered them and said, Verily, verily, I say unto you, <u>Ye seek me, not because ye saw the miracles, but because ye did eat of the loaves and were filled</u>* [referring to the miraculous feeding of the 5000]. *Labour not for the meat which perisheth, but <u>for that meat which endureth unto everlasting life</u>, which the Son of man* [speaking of Himself] *shall give unto you: for <u>him</u> hath God the Father sealed. John 6:26-27*

To reject the message Jesus proclaimed when he was upon the earth was to also reject the message of God the Father in whose name he spoke. For this reason Jesus told them that their refusal to believe what the Father had told them before in the Holy Scriptures concerning his coming would be their condemnation.

> *But I* [Jesus] *know you, that ye have not the love of God in you. I am come in my Father's name, and ye receive me not: if another shall come in his own name, him ye will receive. How can ye believe, which receive honour one of another, and seek not the honour that cometh from God only? Do not think that I will accuse you to the Father: <u>there is one that accuseth you, even Moses</u>* [who wrote God's Law], <u>*in whom ye trust. For had ye believed Moses, ye would have believed me: for he wrote of me*</u>. *John 5:42-46*

As a matter of fact, Jesus warned that only those who were willing to be taught of his Father would be drawn by God to him for salvation.

> *<u>No man can come to me, except the Father which</u> <u>hath sent me draw him</u>: and I will raise him up at the last day. It is written in the prophets, And they shall be all taught of God. <u>Every man therefore</u> <u>that hath heard, and hath learned of the Father,</u> <u>cometh to me</u>. John 6:44-45*

The Significance of Jesus' Sinlessness to be Our Savior

Jesus could not be the promised Savior of the world unless he himself was sinless during his sojourn on earth. John the Baptist introduced Jesus to Israel as the Lamb of God.

> *Behold the <u>Lamb of God</u>, which taketh away the sin of the world. John 1:29*

As God had always required sacrificial lambs to be spotless or without any deficiencies, the Bible describes Jesus as being the ultimate fulfillment of God's requirement.

> *How much more shall the blood of Christ, who through the eternal Spirit* [the Holy Spirit] *<u>offered himself without spot to God</u>, purge your conscience from dead works* [or the need to present animal sacrifices] *to serve the living God? Hebrews 9:14*

> *Forasmuch as ye know that ye were not redeemed with corruptible things, as silver and gold, . . . but with the precious blood of Christ, <u>as of a lamb</u> <u>without blemish and without spot</u>. 1 Peter 1:18-19*

When Jesus was brought to trial by his enemies, they sought all night to find something with which to charge him, and they could not.

> *Now the chief priests, and elders, and all the council, sought false witness against Jesus, to put him to death. But found none: yea, though many false witnesses came, yet found they none . . . [two witnesses to agree]. Matthew 26:59-60*

When Jesus was brought before Pilate who judged him, he told the crowd outside that he could find no fault in Jesus.

> *Pilate therefore went forth again, and saith unto them, Behold, I bring him forth to you, that ye may know that I find no fault in him. John 19:4*

This was in accordance with what the prophet Isaiah had said about the coming Christ over five hundred years before Jesus was placed upon trial.

> *But he was wounded for our transgressions, he was bruised for our iniquities: the chastisement of our peace [with God] was upon him; and with his stripes we are healed. Isaiah 53:5*

The final act of obedience to God was when Jesus voluntarily went to the cross to fulfill the will of his heavenly Father, in order that we might be saved.

> *Who [Jesus] being in the form of God, thought it not robbery to be equal with God: But made himself of no reputation, and took upon him the form of a servant, and was made in the likeness of men: And being found in fashion as a man, he humbled himself, and became obedient unto*

death, even the death of the cross. *Philippians 2:6-8*

Thus through the sufferings Jesus experienced while living upon this earth, though he was God's divine Son and therefore sinless in his divine nature, he never sinned as a man. He therefore qualified himself to save those who turn in faith to him for salvation.

> *Though he were a Son* [or the divine Son of God], *yet learned he obedience by the things which he suffered; And being made perfect, he became the author of eternal salvation unto all that obey him* [in turning to him for salvation]. *Hebrews 5:9*

It is important to note that the kind of life Jesus lived when he was growing up as a man, and the kind of ministry he had here on earth, was just as important to our salvation as his death on the cross for our sins. For apart from this historical essential truth about Jesus Christ of Nazareth, the Gospel of Christ would not be "Good News."

Illustrative Chart of Jesus' Life and Ministry

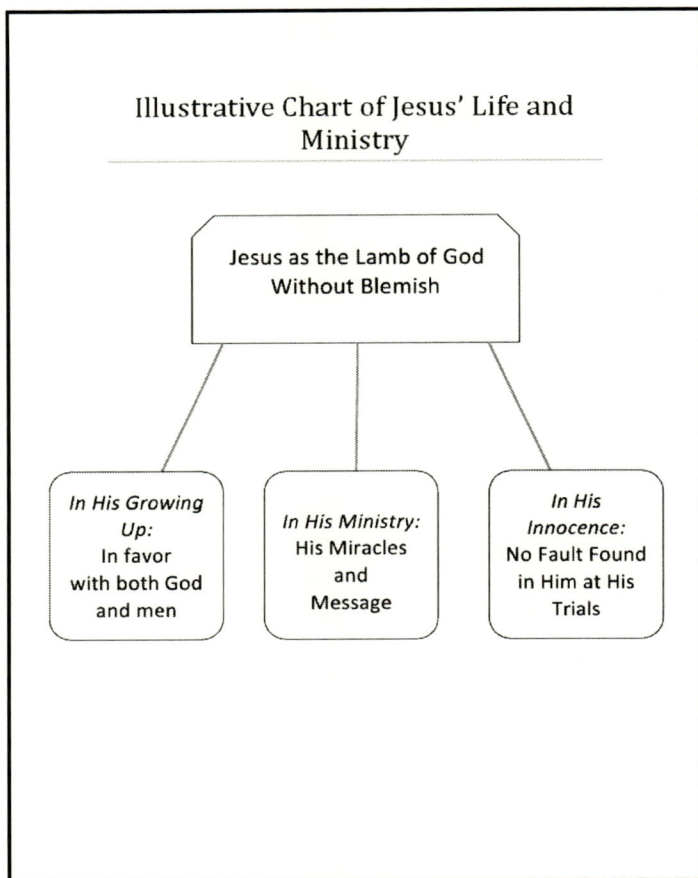

Illustrative Chart of Jesus' Life and Ministry

Jesus as the Lamb of God Without Blemish

In His Growing Up:
In favor with both God and men

In His Ministry:
His Miracles and Message

In His Innocence:
No Fault Found in Him at His Trials

CHAPTER FOUR
WHAT ABOUT JESUS' DEATH?

Introduction

The Roman government practiced a cruel form of execution of its non-citizens in order to put fear in the hearts of the inhabitants of the nations they had conquered. That form of execution was crucifixion. Others had been crucified by the Romans before Jesus. In fact, two others were crucified with Jesus, one on his left hand and one on his right. But the death of Jesus was most unique. In this chapter we will examine the miracles that occurred as Jesus was dying on the cross, as well as the significance of Christ's death on the cross.

The Miracles of Christ's Death on the Cross

The Prophecy of His Crucifixion

Around a thousand years prior to Christ's death on the cross, his crucifixion was foretold before governments executed in this manner. Through the inspiration of the Holy Spirit, King David foretold the crucifixion of the Christ who would come forth from his loins to rule the world.

He foretold the agony Christ would suffer; the pulling apart of his joints as he would struggle to breathe, the intense thirst as a result, and the piercing of his hands and his feet.

> *I am poured out like water, and <u>all my bones are</u>*
> *<u>out of joint</u>: my heart is like wax; it is melted*
> *in the midst of my bowels. My strength is dried*
> *up like a potsherd; and my <u>tongue cleaveth to</u>*
> *<u>my jaws</u>* [intense thirst]*; and thou* [God] *hast*
> *brought me into the dust of death. For dogs have*
> *compassed me: the assembly of the wicked have*
> *inclosed me: <u>they pierced my hands and my feet</u>.*
> *Psalm 22:14-16*

And David's prophecy came to pass for Jesus of Nazareth.

> *But they* [the Israelites in Jerusalem at that time]
> *cried out, Away with him, crucify him. Pilate saith*
> *unto them, Shall I crucify your King? The chief*
> *priests answered, We have no king but Caesar.*
> *They delivered he him therefore unto them to be*
> *crucified. And they took Jesus and led him away.*
> *And he bearing his cross went forth into a place*
> *called the place of a skull, which is called in the*
> *Hebrew Golgotha: <u>Where they crucified him, and</u>*
> *<u>two others with him, on either side one, and Jesus</u>*
> *<u>in the midst</u>. John 19:15-18*

> *After this, Jesus knowing that all things were*
> *now accomplished, that the <u>scripture</u> [or Old*
> *Testament] <u>might be fulfilled, saith, I thirst</u>. John*
> *19:28*

The prophecy of His Garments

King David also foretold of the stripping of Christ's garments from him as he was being crucified, and of the casting of lots for those garments.

> *I may tell all my bones: they look and stare upon me* [because his garments have been stripped from him]. *They part my garments among them, and cast lots upon my vesture. Psalm 22:17-18*

And just as God had foretold through the mouth of His servant David, that is exactly what happened according to eye witness testimony.

> *And they crucified him* [Jesus], *and parted his garments, casting lots: that it might be fulfilled which was spoken by the prophet, They parted my garments among them, and upon my vesture did they cast lots. Matthew 27:35*

The Prophecy of What His Enemies Would Say

Because God knows all things before they happen, He foretold through king David what the enemies of Christ would say as they watched him being crucified.

> *All they that see me* [the Christ] *laugh me to scorn: they shoot out the lip, they shake the head, saying, He trusted on the LORD that he would deliver him, seeing he delighted in him. Psalm 22:7-8*

And by eye witness testimony, that is exactly what occurred.

*And they that passed by <u>reviled him, wagging
their heads</u> . . . <u>He trusted in God, let him deliver
him now</u>, if he will have him . . . Matthew 27:39,43*

The Prophecy of His Cry

King David, in the same Psalm, foretold what Christ
would cry out while being crucified.

*<u>My God, my God, why has thou forsaken me</u>?
Why art thou so far from helping me, and from
the words of my roaring [or grief stricken cry]?
Psalm 22:1*

An amazing thing happened when Jesus was crucified.
At noon when the sunlight should have been at its bright-
est, God caused darkness to come upon the area where Jesus
was being crucified. This was for two reasons: <u>first</u>, because
Jesus had taken upon him the sins of the world, and God
could not look upon sin; and <u>second</u>, because David foretold
the circumstances in which Christ would cry out.

*O my God, <u>I cry in the daytime, but thou hearest
not; and in the night season, and am not silent.
But thou art holy</u>, O thou that inhabitest the
praises of Israel. Psalm 22:2-3*

And that is exactly what happened.

*Now from the sixth hour [noon, Jewish time] <u>there
was darkness over all the land unto the ninth hour</u>
[3:00 p.m.]. And about the ninth hour <u>Jesus cried
with a loud voice</u>, saying, Eli, Eli, lama sabach-
thani? That is to say, <u>My God, my God, why has
thou forsaken me</u>? Matthew 27:45-46*

Jesus did not quote the remaining verses of Psalm 22, but he wanted everyone watching to know that he was fulfilling in his death on the cross what king David had foretold hundreds of years earlier!

The Dismissal of His Human Spirit

While crucifixion was intended for death, Jesus did not die at the hands of men. He died voluntarily by dismissing his human spirit from his body. This a mere man cannot do, but the Son of God did!

> *And when Jesus had cried with a loud voice, he said, Father, into thy hands I commend my spirit: and having said thus, <u>he gave up the ghost</u>* [or his human spirit]. *Luke 23:46*

The Earthquake

As soon as Jesus dismissed his spirit from his body, God caused a powerful earthquake to occur that caused rocks to split apart, graves to be opened, and the tremendous veil in the Temple to be ripped apart from top-to-bottom.

> *Jesus, when he had cried again with a loud voice, yielded up the ghost. And behold, the <u>veil of the temple was rent in twain</u>* [in two] *<u>from the top to the bottom; and the earth did quake, and the rocks rent; And the graves were</u> opened* . . . *Matthew 27:50-51*

The centurion or Roman military commander in charge of the execution was so impressed by what he saw and heard, that he and some of the soldiers with him came to believe that Jesus was the Son of God.

43

Now when <u>the centurion, and they that were with him</u>, watching Jesus, saw the earthquake, and those things that were done, they feared greatly, saying , <u>Truly this was the Son of God</u>. Matthew 27:54

The Blood and Water

The Jewish religious rulers did not want the bodies of Jesus and the thieves left hanging on the cross at the time when the Passover would begin. So they convinced Pilate to see to it that his soldiers hasten death. In order to do so, they broke the legs of the two thieves beside Jesus in order to cause them to die quicker. But when they came to Jesus, and he appeared to already be dead, instead of breaking his legs, they thrust a spear into the side of his chest area. And what came out was astonishing, in that it was both water and blood distinctive from each other.

But one of the soldiers with a spear pierced his side, and <u>forthwith came there out blood and water</u>. John 19:34

Some might attribute this to being a natural consequence of death, in that clear fluid builds in the chest cavity after death. That being true, it would still appear to the viewer as bloody water (or watery blood) gushing forth from an open wound. John takes the time to point out that blood and water came out at the same time, and were clearly distinct from each other as being both blood and pure running water. John wrote that he himself saw it and wanted any doubters to know that what he saw was true. This would indicate that the apostle John thought this to not be a natural occurrence, but indeed a miracle to be recorded.

> *And he that saw it* [John himself] <u>*bare record,*</u>
> *and his record is true: and he knoweth that he*
> *saith true, <u>that ye might believe</u>. John 19:35*

It was not necessary for blood and water to exit the body
of Jesus in order to prove that he was dead. For John writes
that the soldiers already knew he was dead, and for that
reason did not break his legs (John 19:31-33). John says he
wrote down what he saw in order that those who were not
there might believe that Jesus is the divine Son of God.

> <u>*But these are written, that ye might believe that*</u>
> <u>*Jesus is the Son of God;*</u> *and that believing ye*
> *might have life through his name. John 20:31*

If indeed this was a miracle, and Jesus was already dead
(having dismissed his spirit from his body on the tree), who
caused this miracle to occur? John answers this question in
another of his epistles.

> *Who is he that overcometh* [the condemnation
> of] *the world, but <u>he that believeth that Jesus is*</u>
> <u>*the Son of God*</u>. *This is he that came by water*
> *and blood, even Jesus Christ; <u>not by water only,*</u>
> <u>*but by water and blood*</u>. *And <u>it is the Spirit that*</u>
> <u>*beareth witness*</u>, *because the Spirit is truth. 1*
> *John 5:5-6*

The apostle John points out that it was the Holy Spirit who
caused both water and blood to come out of his body on the
cross as a miracle to prove that Jesus was not just another man,
but was indeed the divine Son of God. The shed blood would
be the basis for forgiveness of sins, and the water with the blood
symbolized the cleansing of the sinner because of the blood.

The Significance of Christ's Death on the Cross

He only had to Die Once!

When Adam and Eve first sinned, the Lord had warned them that they would die that very day. When the Lord came to the Garden, after Adam and Eve had sinned, Adam hid because he was afraid. But in God's mercy, the Lord caused an animal (probably a lamb) to be slain and die in their place in order that He might extend their life. He then clothed them with the skins of the animal that had been slain for a reminder to them that forgiveness is only made possible by a blood sacrifice that God would accept, rather than any offering a sinner might bring to God as a result of the works of his own hands (Read Genesis, chapters two and three).

Adam and Eve taught their children this truth about God's requirement for forgiveness. Yet when their first two sons brought a sacrifice to God, Cain chose to bring an offering of his own hands to God rather than a blood sacrifice. In contrast, his younger brother Abel brought the blood sacrifice that his parents had taught him to bring. The Scripture records that God accepted Abel's sacrifice, and rejected Cain's (Read Genesis, chapter four).

Even though the animal blood sacrifices extended the sinner's life for a while, mankind still died because they could not offer a blood sacrifice to God that would be valuable enough for them to receive eternal life. Thus they were taught from the beginning to look in faith to a sacrifice God would one day provide that would save them from the penalty of their sins forever. Abraham and David were examples of having this kind of faith in a blood atonement God would provide whereby they could be justified for salvation; that is, declared to be righteous in the sight of God to receive eternal life.

> *For what saith the scripture? Abraham believed God, and it was counted unto him for righteousness. . . . Even as David also describeth the blessedness of the man, unto whom God imputeth* [or credits with] *righteousness without works, saying, Blessed are they whose iniquities are forgiven, and whose sins are covered* [or atoned for through blood sacrifice]. *Blessed is the man to whom the Lord will not impute sin. Romans 4:3, 6-8*

The writer of the book of Hebrews points out that the most holy animal blood sacrifice the Israelites could offer to God for forgiveness of sins, had to be renewed once a year. This is because the blood of a bull or a goat was not valuable enough to provide eternal forgiveness of sins.

> *But in those sacrifices there is a remembrance again made of sins every year. For it is not possible that the blood of bulls and of goats should take away sins* [permanently]. *Hebrews 10:3-4*

But now that Jesus has come, those who are made holy in the sight of God through the blood of Jesus are perfected forever in God's sight.

> *For by one offering* [Jesus Christ's one blood sacrifice on the cross] *he* [God] *hath perfected forever them that are sanctified* [or made a holy people in the sight of God]. *Hebrews 10:14*

Because Jesus has presented the blood he shed on the cross in heaven, the spirits of believers are now made perfect in the sight of God whereby they are now permitted to enter God's presence in heaven. Thus the blood of Jesus is far more valuable than the blood sacrifice Abel offered in the beginning.

> *But ye are come unto Mount Zion* [in heaven],
> *and unto the city of the living God, <u>the heavenly</u>*
> *<u>Jerusalem,</u> and to an innumerable company of*
> *angels, To the general assembly and church of*
> *the firstborn, which are written in heaven, and*
> *to God the Judge of all, and to the <u>spirits of just</u>*
> *<u>men made perfect, And to Jesus the mediator of</u>*
> *<u>the new covenant, and to the blood of sprinkling,</u>*
> *<u>that speaketh better things than that of Abel</u>.*
> *Hebrews 12:22-24*

Since Jesus died on the cross, he has never had to come into the world to die again, because his blood is valuable enough in the sight of God to save sinners once for all. The reason for this is the truth that when Jesus shed his precious blood, it was not just the blood of a good man, but it was the blood of God Himself! The apostle Paul emphasized this truth to the elders of the church at Ephesus.

> *Take heed therefore unto yourselves, and to all*
> *the flock* [the local church at the city of Ephesus],
> *over the which the Holy Ghost* [or Holy Spirit]
> *hath made you overseers, to feed* [with spiri-
> tual food from God's Word] *the <u>church of God,</u>*
> *<u>which he</u>* [Paul referring to Jesus as God] *<u>hath</u>*
> *<u>purchased with his own blood</u>. Acts 20:28*

The Two-Fold Benefit of Christ's Death on the Cross

God had the nation Israel perform animal blood sacrifices in order for them to understand what Christ would have to do when he came into the world as the Lamb of God. First, the blood was shed and presented to God for forgiveness of sins. Second, the body of the animal was then burned completely on the Altar of Burnt Offering.

In the same manner, Jesus not only shed his precious blood to provide eternal forgiveness of sins and eternal life, but he also condemned the sin nature with which we are all born in his own body on the tree. All of mankind, whether male or female, are born with a nature to sin that has been passed down from the first man who sinned, Adam.

> *Wherefore, <u>as by one man</u>* [Adam] *<u>sin entered into the world</u>, and death by sin; and so death passed upon all men, for that all have sinned.*
> *Romans 5:12*

So when Jesus died on the cross, he not only paid for the sins committed by all of mankind since Adam, but he also condemned our natural propensity to sin in his own body on the tree in order to save us from this sin nature with which we were born.

> *Knowing this, that <u>our old man</u>* [or sin nature passed down from Adam] *<u>is crucified with him</u>, that the <u>body of sin might be destroyed</u>, that <u>henceforth we should not serve sin</u>. Romans 6:6*

In the day of resurrection, all of those who have placed their trust in what Jesus did for them on the cross, will be delivered forever from the sinful nature with which we are born. Otherwise, God could not allow us to enter the new heavens and earth He will one day create.

> *For our conversation* [or citizenship] *is in heaven; from whence also we look for the Saviour, the Lord Jesus Christ: <u>Who shall change our vile body</u>, that it may be fashioned like unto his glorious body* [referring to being made like the Lord

Jesus in a sinless resurrected body]. . .

Christians celebrate this two-fold benefit of Christ's death on the cross when they participate in Communion or the Lord's Supper. The unleavened bread which is eaten represents what Jesus did in his crucified body to deliver us from the sin nature with which we are born, and the grape juice represents what Jesus did to provide a payment God would accept in his shed blood for forgiveness of sins we commit in yielding to our nature to sin.

The following chart will help to portray the significance of Christ's death on the cross.

Illustrative Chart of the Two-Fold Benefit of Christ's Death on the Cross

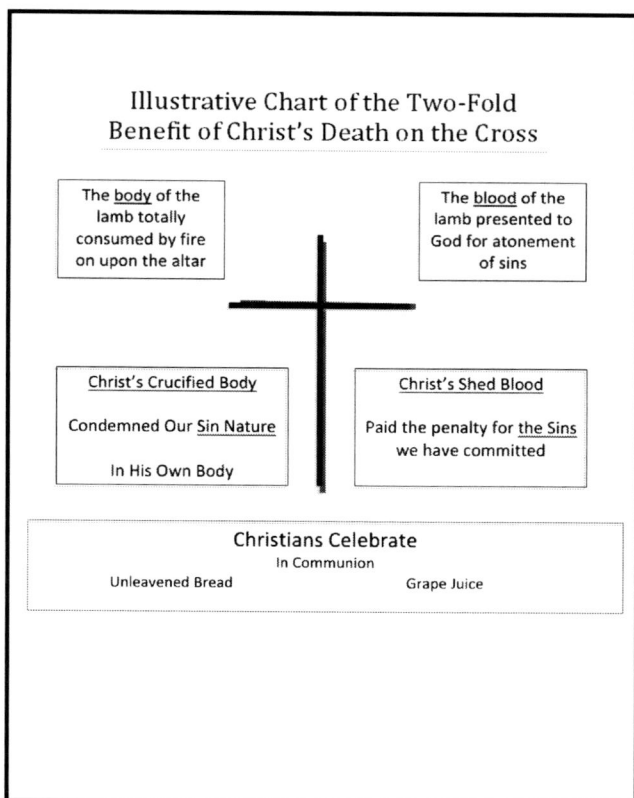

Illustrative Chart of the Two-Fold
Benefit of Christ's Death on the Cross

The body of the lamb totally consumed by fire on upon the altar

The blood of the lamb presented to God for atonement of sins

Christ's Crucified Body

Condemned Our Sin Nature

In His Own Body

Christ's Shed Blood

Paid the penalty for the Sins we have committed

Christians Celebrate
In Communion
Unleavened Bread   Grape Juice

CHAPTER FIVE
WHAT ABOUT JESUS' RESURRECTION?

Introduction

Additional evidence that Jesus of Nazareth is the divine Son of God is the historical fact that Jesus rose from the dead by the power of God before his body could corrupt in the grave. It is the resurrection of Jesus Christ that separates Christianity from all other religions in the world. In this chapter we will examine the <u>historical proofs</u> that Jesus did indeed rise from the dead on the third day as he himself had promised, and then examine the <u>significance of his resurrection</u> for those who put their faith and trust in him.

Historical Proofs that Jesus rose from the dead

His Empty Tomb

Jesus had foretold his death and resurrection the third day from the beginning of his ministry.

> *Jesus answered and said unto them, <u>Destroy this temple, and in three days I will raise it up</u>. Then said the Jews, Forty and six years was this temple in building, and wilt thou rear it up*

*in three days? <u>But he spake of the temple of his</u>
<u>body. When therefore he was risen from the dead,</u>
<u>his disciples remembered that he had said this</u>
<u>unto them; and they believed the scripture, and</u>
<u>the word which Jesus said</u>. John 2:19-22*

The Scripture to which the apostle John refers is God's promise that the Christ, or Holy One, would live such a perfect life, that God would not permit his body to corrupt in the grave and go back to the dust from which it was made. King David prophesied this around a thousand years prior to the coming of Jesus Christ of Nazareth.

For thou [God] *wilt not leave my soul in hell* [or the underworld]*; neither <u>wilt thou suffer</u>* [or allow] *<u>thine Holy One to see corruption</u>. Psalm 16:10*

When Jesus died on the cross and was buried, his enemies did not believe his promise. They thought that his disciples might try to steal his body before the third day, and then proclaim that he had risen as he said to keep the "religious cult" alive. So they convinced Pilate to seal the tomb with a heavy stone in front of the grave (it being above ground), and place a Roman guard in front of it to make sure that did not happen. But God overruled the schemes of man, as recorded by eye witness testimony, on the morning of the third day.

In the end of the Sabbath [Saturday]*, as it began to dawn toward the first day of the week* [Sunday morning]*, came Mary Magdalene and the other to see the sepulchre. And, behold, <u>there was</u>
<u>a great earthquake: for the angel of the Lord</u>
<u>descended from heaven, and came and rolled</u>
<u>back the stone from the door, and sat upon it</u>. His countenance was like lightning, and his raiment*

white as snow: And <u>for fear of him the keepers</u> [or Roman soldiers guarding the tomb] <u>did shake, and became as dead men</u> [that is, they passed out and fell to the ground]. *Matthew 28:1-4*

The reason the angel rolled away the stone was not to let Jesus out, but to allow the women in to see that he was not there. He had already risen.*And the angel answered and said unto the women, Fear not ye: for I know that ye seek Jesus, which was crucified. <u>He is not here: for he is risen, as he said. Come, see the place where the Lord lay</u> [or had been laid in the tomb]. Matthew 28:5-6*

<u>His Many Appearances</u>

Jesus appeared often for the next forty days to his disciples. . .

He appeared first on the Sunday morning of his resurrection to Mary Magdalene in the garden area where the tomb was. John 20:11-16
He appeared to Peter later that morning or early afternoon. Luke 24:34
He appeared to two of his disciples that afternoon on the road to Emmaus. Luke 24:13-35
He appeared to women with Mary Magdalene as they went to tell the other disciples in the upper room. Matthew 28:9-10
He appeared to eleven of his disciples, minus Thomas. John 20:19-23
He appeared eight days later to all twelve of his disciples who became his apostles, this time with Thomas present. John 20:24-29 and 1 Corinthians 15:5
He then appeared to more than five hundred men at the same time in Galilee, many of whom were still alive

and could testify at the time Paul wrote his epistle to the Corinthians on his third missionary journey. 1 Corinthians 15:6

He appeared to James, his half brother [who later became one of the chief apostles and wrote the epistle of James in the New Testament]. 1 Corinthians 15:7

He appeared to even more afterwards. 1 Corinthians 15:7

He appeared, last of all, to the apostle Paul after Jesus had visibly ascended into heaven. 1 Corinthians 15:8

Too Many Died

How could the testimony of so many people be wrong, especially since many of them died for their testimony? Eleven of the twelve apostles were martyred for their testimony, and John suffered exile by the Roman government on the Isle of Patmos. Revelation 1:9

The Significance of Jesus's Resurrection for Those Who Place Their Trust in Him

We Are Made Acceptable to God in Christ

Other people have come back to life when they had been pronounced dead, but later died again and their bodies went back to dust. For this is the curse that God had placed upon the first man, Adam, for his sin.

> *In the sweat of thy face shalt thou eat bread, till thou return unto the ground; for out of it was thou taken: for dust thou art, and unto dust shalt thou return. Genesis 3:19*

In the process of returning to dust, the body begins to stink by the fourth day. Martha reminded Jesus of this about her brother who had died, and it was the fourth day.

> *Jesus said, Take ye away the stone. Martha, the sister of him that was dead, saith unto him, Lord, by this time he stinketh: for he hath been dead four days. John 11:39*

But Jesus rose from the dead on the third day; having been in the tomb long enough to prove he really died, but before corruption could begin. As noted above, this proved that Jesus of Nazareth was the Holy One whom David had foretold hundreds of years before. The fact that Jesus rose from the dead on the third day before his body could corrupt was used by the apostle Peter to proclaim fifty days later that Jesus was indeed the Christ, and three thousand Jews changed their minds and believed.

> *Men and brethren, let me freely speak unto you of the patriarch David, That he is both dead and buried, and his sepulchre is with us unto this day* [proving that he was not the one of whom David spoke]. *Therefore being a prophet, and knowing that God had sworn with an oath to him, that of the fruit of his loins, according to the flesh, he would raise up Christ to sit on his throne; He* [David] *seeing this before spake of the resurrection of Christ, that his soul was not left in hell* [or the underworld], *neither his flesh did see corruption. This Jesus* [whom they had just crucified] *hath God raised up, whereof we all are witnesses. Acts 2:29-32*

The apostle Paul proclaimed that Christ's resurrection the third day proved he died for our sins and not for his own.

For I delivered unto you first of all that which I also received, how that <u>Christ died for our sins</u> according to the scriptures [Old Testament], *And that he was buried* [proving that the same Jesus who died on the cross was the same who then rose again], *and that <u>he rose again the third day according to the scriptures</u>* [that foretold of Christ not being permitted by God to corrupt in the grave]. *1 Corinthians 15:3-4*

Paul proclaimed that, being raised from the dead before Christ's body could corrupt, proved that sinners could be made acceptable to God if they put their faith and trust in the goodness of Christ, whereas they could never be made acceptable by their own works under the Mosaic Law.

And as concerning that he [God] *raised him up from the dead, now no more to return to corruption, he said on this wise, I will give you the sure mercies of David* [or the promises God made to David concerning the coming Christ]. *Wherefore he saith in another psalm, Thou shalt not suffer* [or allow] *thine Holy One to see corruption. For David, after he served his own generation by the will of God, fell on sleep, and was laid unto his fathers, and saw corruption. <u>But he</u>* [Jesus], <u>*whom God raised again, saw no corruption. Be it known unto you therefore, men and brethren, that <u>through this man</u>* [Jesus] *<u>is preached unto you the forgiveness of sins: And by him all that believe</u>* [in him, Jesus] *<u>are justified from all things</u>* [all their sins], *from which ye could not be justified by the law of Moses* [or by their own attempts to earn God's eternal favor in keeping the Mosaic Law]. *Acts 13:34-39*

Our Bodies Will Be Changed

We will be raised immortal through Christ.

Who [God] hath saved us, and called us with an holy calling, not according to our works, but according to his own purpose and grace, which was given us in Christ Jesus before the world began, But is now made manifest by the appearing of our Saviour Jesus Christ, <u>who hath abolished death, and hath brought life and immortality to light through the gospel</u>. 2 Timothy 1:9-10

We will be raised to never sin or suffer the consequences of sin again.

And God shall wipe away all tears from their eyes; and there shall <u>be no more death, neither sorrow, nor crying ,neither shall there be any more pain</u>: for the former things are passed away. Revelation 21:4

We will be given a body capable of living forever in the new heavens and the new earth.

And as we have borne the image of the earthy, <u>we shall also bear the image of the heavenly</u>. Now this I say, brethren, that <u>flesh and blood</u> [as it is now] <u>cannot inherit the kingdom of God; neither doth corruption inherit incorruption</u>. 1 Corinthians 15:49-50

Illustrative Chart of Christ's Resurrection Appearances

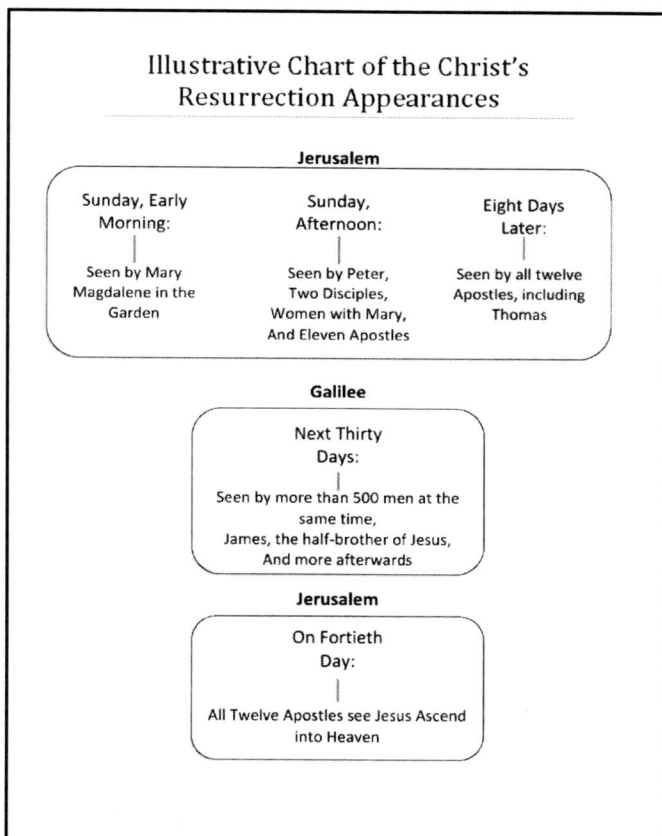

Illustrative Chart of the Christ's Resurrection Appearances

Jerusalem

Sunday, Early Morning:	Sunday, Afternoon:	Eight Days Later:
Seen by Mary Magdalene in the Garden	Seen by Peter, Two Disciples, Women with Mary, And Eleven Apostles	Seen by all twelve Apostles, including Thomas

Galilee

Next Thirty Days:

Seen by more than 500 men at the same time,
James, the half-brother of Jesus,
And more afterwards

Jerusalem

On Fortieth Day:

All Twelve Apostles see Jesus Ascend into Heaven

CHAPTER SIX
WHAT ABOUT JESUS' ASCENSION INTO HEAVEN?

Introduction

When Jesus rose from the dead, his body was changed: from that which is natural to that which is spiritual; from that which is earthly to that which is heavenly; from that which is dishonorable to that which is honorable; from that which is weak to that which is powerful; from that which is mortal to that which is immortal; from that which is corruptible to that which is incorruptible. And that is the kind of body Jesus will one day give to all those who put their faith and trust in him.

> *So also is the resurrection of the dead. It is sown in corruption; it is raised in incorruption: It is sown in dishonor; it is raised in glory* [or honor]*: it is sown in weakness; it is raised in power: It is sown a natural body; it is raised a spiritual body. . .*
>
> *The first man* [Adam] *is of the earth, earthy: the second man is the Lord* [Jesus] *from heaven. As is the earthy, such are they also that are earthy: and as is the heavenly, such are they also that are heavenly. And as we have borne the image*

of the earthy, we shall also bear the image of the heavenly.

Now this I say, brethren, that flesh and blood cannot inherit the kingdom of God; neither doth corruption inherit incorruption. 1 Corinthians 15:42-50

In his resurrected body Jesus was not always immediately recognizable, though he still retained the wounds in his hands, feet, and side to prove to doubters like Thomas that it was he. Jesus could appear and disappear at will. He could ascend into heaven and into the heart of the earth. He no longer had the limitations he experienced prior to his death on the cross. His was now a glorified immortal body, and it was in his new resurrected body that he first appeared to Mary Magdalene.

Jesus' Ascension into Heaven to Present His Blood

Mary Magdalene had come back to the garden after she and other women had seen the empty tomb early the Sunday morning after Jesus was crucified. She thought perhaps that someone had stolen the body of Jesus and stood weeping outside the tomb. Then she saw what she thought was the keeper of the garden where the tomb was located, and through her tears she begged him to tell her where his body might have been taken. It is then that Jesus spoke to her by her name, and she would have run towards him, no doubt, with both surprise and joy; but Jesus told her not to touch him!

Jesus saith unto her, <u>Touch me not</u>; <u>for I am not yet ascended to my Father</u>: But go to my brethren, and <u>say unto them, I ascend unto my Father</u>, and your Father; and to my God, and your God. John 20:17

61

For those who are not familiar with the Bible, the three persons of the Holy Trinity (Father, Son Jesus, and the Holy Spirit) address each other as being both Lord and God. This is because they are one God in divine essence, yet eternally existent in three persons. So it is not unusual for Jesus to refer to the heavenly Father who sent him into the world as his God. But why did Jesus command Mary to not touch him?

The answer is that the Law of God, as set forth in the book of Leviticus, required that no one common could touch the body of the sacrifice while the blood was in the process of being presented to God within the Tabernacle. Over again the Lord warned the Israelites that if they violated His strict rules regarding the animal sin offerings, they would suffer instantaneous death. The Scriptures use the words, "that soul shall be cut off."

The reason Jesus commanded Mary to not touch him was because it was his intent at that time to ascend to his heavenly Father and present his blood sacrifice to God for the remission or forgiveness of sins. God had always required that the blood of the sacrifice be presented to Him by His appointed High Priest, as the payment by which God could justify forgiving sins. Because of the value of the blood of Christ in the Father's sight, Jesus had only to present his blood to God the Father once. For once the blood of Jesus is applied to the sinner's account in heaven, he or she is eternally set free from facing the wrath of God for their sins in the final Day of Judgment.

> *Neither by the blood of goats and calves, but by his own blood he* [Jesus] *entered in once into the holy place* [in heaven], *having obtained eternal redemption for us. Hebrews 9:12*

While God does chastise His children in this life for the sins they commit after they become His children by faith, they will never face His eternal wrath and condemnation because of the value of Christ's blood which has been applied to their account for salvation.

> *For whom the Lord loveth he chasteneth,*
> *and scourgeth every son whom he receiveth.*
> *Hebrews 12:6*

Jesus' Ascension Forty Days Later To Sit On God's Throne

Jesus appeared off and on to his disciples for the next forty days. But on this occasion they actually saw him ascend into heaven with their own eyes.

> *And when he* [Jesus] *had spoken these things,*
> *while they beheld, he was taken up and a cloud*
> *received him out of their sight. Acts 1:9*

The question arises as to whether or not Jesus will reappear. Yes! But two angels told his disciples to not stand around looking for him, but to spread the good news of his death, burial, and resurrection as proof that he is coming again.

> *And while they looked steadfastly toward heaven*
> *as he went up, behold, two men stood by them in*
> *white apparel* [angels]*; Which also said, Ye men*
> *of Galilee, why stand ye gazing up into heaven?*
> *This same Jesus, which is taken up from you into*
> *heaven, shall so come in like manner as ye have*
> *seen him go into heaven. Acts 1:9-11*

Ten days later, on the day of Pentecost, Peter boldly told the Jews in Jerusalem that Jesus had not only been raised from the dead by God in heaven, but that Jesus was now seated at the Father's right hand in heaven as the promised Messiah or Christ.

Therefore let all the house of Israel know assur-
edly, that <u>God hath made that same Jesus</u>, whom
ye have crucified, <u>both Lord and Christ</u>. Acts 2:36

Three thousand Jews were so convicted of not having believed in Jesus, that they asked Peter what they could do to be saved.

Now when they heard this, they were pricked in
their heart, and said unto Peter and to the rest
of the apostles, Men and brethren, what shall we
do? Acts 2:37

They did not want to be judged by God for having rejected Jesus as their Savior! They believed that if Jesus was indeed risen, and seated at the right hand of the Father, he would certainly come back to earth to defeat all those who have opposed him. And indeed, Jesus is coming again, which is the topic of the next chapter.

Illustrative Chart of Two Ascensions of Jesus

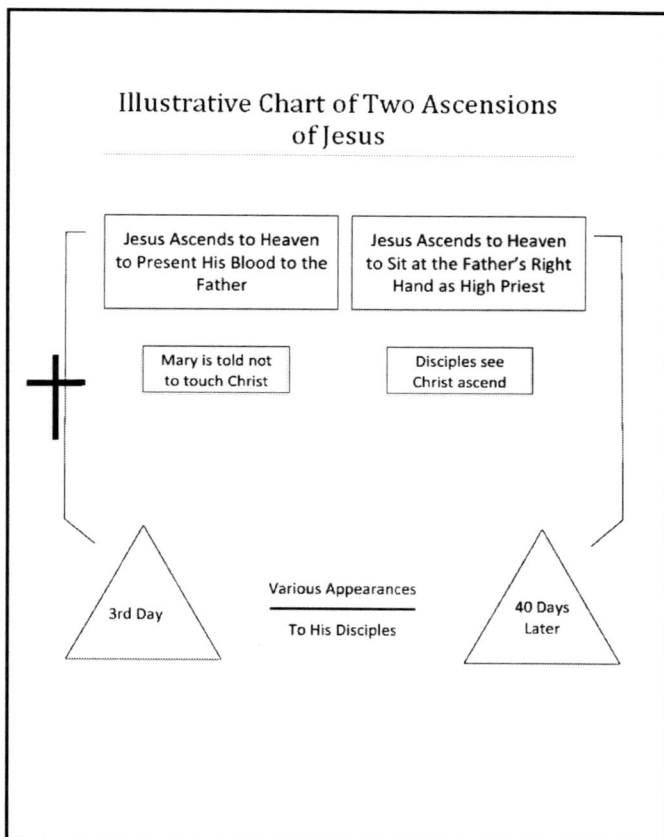

Illustrative Chart of Two Ascensions of Jesus

| Jesus Ascends to Heaven to Present His Blood to the Father | Jesus Ascends to Heaven to Sit at the Father's Right Hand as High Priest |

Mary is told not to touch Christ

Disciples see Christ ascend

3rd Day

Various Appearances

To His Disciples

40 Days Later

CHAPTER SEVEN
WHAT ABOUT JESUS' COMING AGAIN?

Introduction

Yes, Christians believe that Jesus is coming again. Paul wrote the following words to one of the churches he planted on his second missionary journey:

> *For from you sounded out the word of the Lord* [by word of mouth] *not only in Macedonia and Achaia* [or modern day Greece], *but also in every place your faith to God-ward is spread abroad; so that we need not to speak any thing.*

> *For they themselves shew of us* [or demonstrate to us] *what manner of entering in we had unto you, and how ye turned to God from idols to serve the living and true God. And to wait for his Son from heaven, whom he raised from the dead, even Jesus, which delivered us from the wrath to come. 1 Thessalonians 1:8-10*

The coming again of Jesus Christ will come in two phases. He will first come in the air to catch away those who have placed their faith and trust in him from the time of his ascension into heaven, whether they be dead or still living at the time. This is called by theologians the Rapture of the Church.

He will then come a second time to this earth in order to raise all of those who believed in God's Son before he came into this world, even though they did not as yet know what his name would be. He will then defeat all of God's enemies on earth and usher in God's everlasting kingdom as the promised Messiah or Christ.

The Rapture of the Church

The nation of Israel was offered the kingdom of God in their lifetime when Jesus was on the earth. Yet they refused to repent of their sins as a whole, rejected him, and delivered him over to the Gentiles to be crucified. They cried out, *"His blood be on us, and on our children!"* (Matthew 27:25).

After Jesus arose from the dead and ascended into heaven, they were offered the kingdom again if they would repent of their having delivered Christ over to the Gentiles to be crucified (Acts 3:19-21). There were many Jews who did repent, but the nation as a whole did not. So God began a new nation to represent God on earth today, called the Church. This new nation is now composed of individual believing Jews and Gentiles who are now considered by God to be one in Christ. The mystery of what God is doing in this dispensation was first revealed to the apostle Paul.

> *For this cause I Paul, the prisoner of Jesus Christ for you Gentiles, <u>If ye have heard of the dispensa-tion</u>* [or different time period in God's program] *of the grace of God which is given me to you-ward: <u>How that by revelation he made known unto me the mystery</u>* [or information previously not known]; *Ephesians 3:1-3a*

The apostle Paul goes on to say what this mystery is.

(As I wrote afore in few words, Whereby, when ye read, ye may understand my knowledge in the <u>mystery of Christ), Which in other ages was not made known unto the sons of men</u>, as it is now revealed unto his holy apostles and prophets by the Spirit [or Holy Spirit]; <u>*That the Gentiles should be fellowheirs*</u>, [with the Jews] <u>*and of the same body, and partakers of his promise in Christ by the gospel*</u>. *Ephesians 3:3b-6*

Paul identifies this new nation as being Christ's Church.

<u>*And to make all men see what is the fellowship of the mystery*</u>, *which from the beginning of the world hath been hid in God, who created all things by Jesus Christ: To the intent that now unto the principalities and powers in heavenly places might be known <u>by the church</u> the manifold wisdom of God. Ephesians 3:9-10*

The reason I capitalize the word "Church" is to distinguish true believers in Christ today from those who may join a local church, but not really be saved. Those who are truly part of Christ's Church in this dispensation have been given the Holy Spirit to indwell them and guide them in their life for Christ as of the day they are saved. Paul says that it is the assembly of Gentiles and Jews, who are indwelt by the Spirit because of their common faith in Jesus Christ, that makes up the true Church as a holy temple representing God in this dispensation.

Now therefore ye [Gentile believers] *are no more strangers and foreigners, but <u>fellowcitizens</u> with the saints* [Jewish believers], *and of the household of God; <u>And are built upon the foundation</u> of the*

> *apostles and prophets, <u>Jesus Christ himself being</u>*
> *<u>the chief corner stone</u>; In whom all the building*
> *fitly framed together <u>groweth unto an holy temple</u>*
> *in the Lord: In whom ye also are <u>builded together</u>*
> *<u>for an habitation of God through the Spirit</u>* [or
> indwelling Holy Spirit]. *Ephesians 2:19-22*

The true Church of Jesus Christ began suddenly on the Day of Pentecost, when Jesus sent the Holy Spirit from heaven to indwell all believers from that day forth. And just as suddenly as God began the Church, He will suddenly remove the Church from the earth, whether they be dead or living at the time. Paul describes this in his letter to the Thessalonians.

> *For this we say unto you by the word of the Lord,*
> *that we which are alive and remain <u>unto the</u>*
> *<u>coming of the Lord</u> shall not prevent* [or hinder]
> *them which are asleep* [a term for believers who
> have died in the Lord]. *For the Lord himself*
> *shall descend from heaven with a shout, with the*
> *voice of the archangel* [or one of God's ruling
> angels], *and with the trump of God: and the dead*
> *in Christ shall rise first: Then <u>we which are alive</u>*
> *<u>and remain shall be caught up</u>* ["Raptured" in the
> Latin language] *<u>together with them in the clouds,</u>*
> *<u>to meet the Lord in the air: and so shall we ever</u>*
> *<u>be with the Lord</u>. 1 Thessalonians 4:15-17*

The reason the Lord will suddenly snatch believers who are still alive from the earth is to enable them to escape the coming Tribulation which will suddenly hit the nations of the world with no prior warning and no escape. For Paul goes on to say . . .

> *But of the times and the seasons, brethren, ye have no need that I write unto you. For yourselves know perfectly that <u>the day of the Lord so cometh as a thief in the night</u>* [catching men by surprise]. *For when they shall say, Peace and safety; then <u>sudden destruction cometh upon them</u>, as travail* [labor pains] *upon a woman with child; <u>and they shall not escape</u>. 1 Thessalonians 5:1-3*

The promised "day of the Lord" was prophesied in the Old Testament as a terrible outpouring of God's wrath upon the whole world for their sins. This would be a time of God's warning mankind that time is running out for them to repent of their sins before Christ returns to bring God's kingdom rule to earth.

> *Behold , the <u>day of the Lord cometh, cruel both with wrath and fierce anger</u>, to lay the land desolate: and he* [God] *shall destroy the sinners thereof out of it. For the stars of heaven and the constellations thereof shall not give their light to shine. <u>And I</u>* [God] <u>*will punish the world for their evil, and the wicked for their iniquity*</u>*...Isaiah 13:9-11*

This day, of God's outpoured wrath upon the nations for their sin, is called by Jesus a time of tribulation. Because God's children are not appointed to wrath, God will cause those who are part of his Church to escape by being snatched up into heaven to meet the Lord in the air. Since the time of God's wrath could come suddenly at any time, the Rapture of the Church could also come suddenly, and is a blessed truth that should be of great comfort to every believer today. Paul says so twice in 1 Thessalonians 4:18 and 5:11.

I have written information about the Rapture of the Church and the Tribulation before Jesus returns the second time to this earth in order to establish God's kingdom. The book's title is *The Mysterious Disappearance*, and was published by Xulon Press in 2008.

The Return of Christ to This Earth

At the end of the Tribulation period, Jesus Christ himself will return to this earth with his saved and glorified Church to defeat his foes and establish God's kingdom. A final battle will take place as described in the last book of the Bible.

> *And I saw heaven opened, and behold a white horse; and he that sat upon him* [or the horse] *was called Faithful and True* [referring to the Lord Jesus], *and in righteousness he doth judge and make war. His eyes were as a flame of fire, and on his head were many crowns; and he had a name written, that no man knew, but he himself* [referring to a new name God the Father gave to Jesus when he ascended into heaven] *(Philippians 2:9)*.

> *And he was clothed with a vesture dipped in blood* [of his enemies]*: and his name is called the Word of God* [again a reference to another name for Jesus, John 1:1,14]. *And the armies which were in heaven followed him upon white horses* [Christ's glorified Church], *clothed in fine linen, white and clean. And out of his mouth goeth a sharp sword, that with it he should smite the nations: and he shall rule them with a rod of iron: and he treadeth the winepress of the fierceness and wrath of Almighty God. And he hath on his vesture and on his thigh a name written, KING OF KINGS, AND LORD OF LORDS. Revelation 19:11-16.*

71

It will be at this time that Jesus will be anointed King over the earth, and he will reign on the throne of David as promised before by God from the land of Israel. His reign on earth as the Christ was foretold in many passages of the Old Testament. One of the most descriptive is recorded by the prophet Isaiah.

> *And it shall come to pass in the last days, that the mountain of the Lord's house* [or Temple] *shall be established in the top of the mountains, and shall be exalted above the hills; and all nations shall flow into it. And many people shall go and say, Come ye, and let us go up to the mountain of the LORD, to the house* [or Temple in Jerusalem] *of the God of Jacob* [from whom descended the twelve tribes of Israel]; *and he will teach us his ways, and we will walk in his paths: for out of Zion* [the mountain on which the city of Jerusalem sits] *shall go forth the law* [just as Jesus said he would do in his Sermon on the Mount, Matthew 5:17], *and the word of the LORD from Jerusalem. And he* [Jesus as the Christ] *shall judge among the nations, and shall rebuke many people: and they shall beat their swords into plowshares, and their spears into pruninghooks: nation shall not lift up sword against nation, neither shall they learn war any more. Isaiah 2:2-4*

Although Jesus' reign in the kingdom of God will last forever, its first thousand years will be upon this present earth before the Lord causes it to pass away and replace it with a new heavens and a new earth. Six times in seven verses the book of Revelation makes it clear that Jesus' reign on this present earth will last one thousand years prior to God's creation of new heavens and a new earth (compare Revelation 20:1-7 with 21:1). Bible scholars have identified this time period as the Millennium, from the Latin word for "one thousand."

There are many reasons for the Millennium. These are some of those reasons:

- Jesus will fulfill God's promises made to Abraham and his offspring the Jews. God will yet promote the nation of Israel to become the head of the nations, after having first disciplined His people for their national disobedience these many years.
- Jesus will prove in saving and exalting the nation of Israel at this time, that the God of Abraham is the one true God and Creator of us all, both Jews and Gentiles. Thus the whole world will be rebuked for its idolatry and following other gods.
- Jesus will make the land of Israel from which he governs like the former Garden of Eden, to remind mankind of what it was like between God and man before he sinned.
- Jesus will force sinful men still living to obey the moral law of God and conduct themselves as God had intended for man to live since sin entered the world.
- Jesus will reward those believers who lived in obedience after he saved them, as well as dishonor (but not condemn) those who did not.
- Jesus will demonstrate that the true enemy of man is not God, but the Devil or Satan who deceived man into sinning against God and is still doing so.

Most of the prophecies in the Bible yet to be fulfilled concerning the kingdom of God are speaking of Christ's beginning reign upon this earth. This is because it is the Millennial kingdom in which God fulfills His ultimate purpose for Jesus Christ, by whom He created the world, and for whom He created the world.

For by him were all things created, that are in heaven, and that are in earth, visible and invisible, whether they be thrones, or dominions, or principalities, or powers: all <u>*things were created by him, and for him*</u> [speaking of Jesus]. *Colossians 1:16*

And it is only in the final dispensation, called the "dispensation of the fullness of times" by the apostle Paul (Ephesians 1:10), that Jesus will be victorious over all of his foes and take this earth he created in the beginning back under his control. It is only after this that Jesus then causes this world to pass away and creates new heavens and a new earth.

And, Thou, Lord [referring to Jesus], *in the beginning hast laid the foundation of the earth; and the heavens are the works of thine hands:* <u>*they shall perish; but thou remainest; and they all shall wax old as doth a garment; And as a vesture shalt thou fold them up, and they shall be changed*</u>*: but thou art the same, and thy years shall not fail. Hebrews 1:10-12*

The new heavens and earth are described in the last two chapters of the book of Revelation. It is at this time that believers in Christ enter their eternal future, and will forever experience God's kindness towards us in Christ.

But God, who is rich in mercy, for his great love wherewith he loved us, Even when we were dead in sins, hath he quickened us [or made us alive] *together with Christ, (by grace ye are saved;) And hath raised us up together in heavenly places in Christ Jesus:* <u>*That in the ages to come he might shew the exceeding riches of his grace*</u>

74

in his kindness toward us through Christ Jesus: For by grace [or the favor of God] *are ye saved* [from the penalty of your sins] *through faith [in Jesus Christ]; and that* [being saved is] *not of yourselves: it is the gift of God: not of works* [or anything we might do to save ourselves], *lest any man should boast* [in themselves rather than Jesus]. *Ephesians 2:4-9*

Does this excite you? Wouldn't you like to know for sure that this will be your eternal future? The Bible says you can know, provided you obey God's command regarding your response to Him and His plan for you in Christ. That is the subject of the next chapter.

Illustrative Chart of the Coming of Jesus Christ

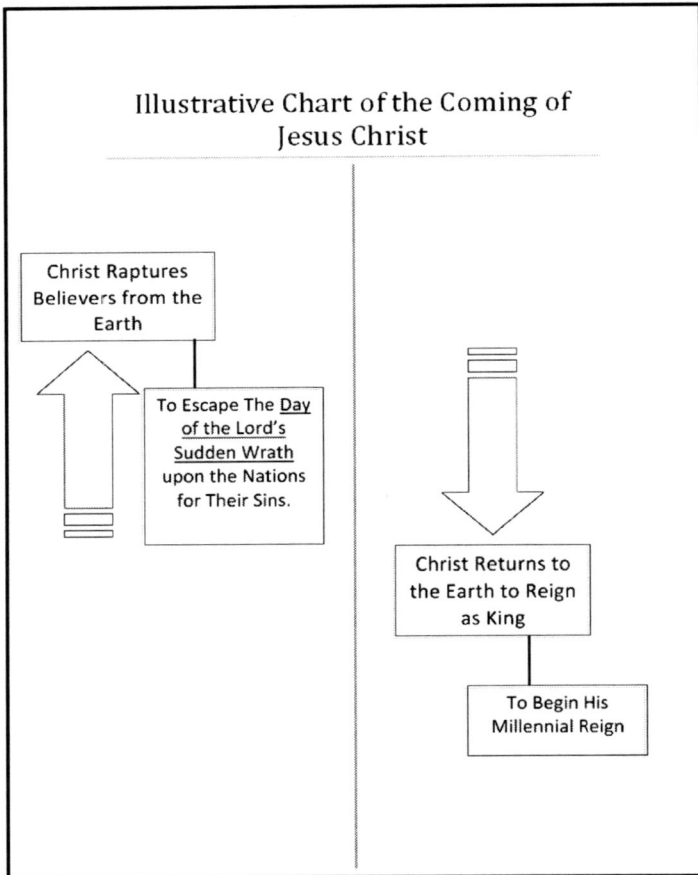

Illustrative Chart of the Coming of Jesus Christ

Christ Raptures Believers from the Earth

To Escape The <u>Day of the Lord's Sudden Wrath</u> upon the Nations for Their Sins.

Christ Returns to the Earth to Reign as King

To Begin His Millennial Reign

CHAPTER EIGHT
WHAT ABOUT YOUR RESPONSE?

†

Introduction

When Jesus ascended into heaven to sit down at the right hand of the Father, it was in order to intercede forgiveness of sins on behalf of sinners who placed their faith and trust in him alone for their salvation, their faith in his righteousness in the sight of God the Father to intercede for sinners, and their faith in the value of his precious blood to save them from eternal condemnation for the sins they have committed. Prior to Christ's coming into the world, God had established through the Levitical animal sacrifices what would be necessary to obtain forgiveness of sins.

We will look at the process God required for forgiveness of sins under the Levitical system of the Mosaic Law, look at how that procedure applies to our response to what Jesus has done for us, and then the urgency of our response to Christ.

The Process God Required for Forgiveness of Sins

For many years, through observing the Levitical priest's function as required by God, the nation of Israel was taught the procedure by which to receive forgiveness of sins.

- The sinner approached God's designated place of sacrifice with an animal sacrifice that God would accept
- The sinner would confess his sin in repentance towards God.
- The sinner would then take a knife and cut the neck of the animal being sacrificed in his place, for the "wages of sin is death."

For the <u>life of the flesh is in the blood</u>: and I [God] *have given it to you upon the altar* [of sacrifice] *to make an atonement [or covering] for your souls, for <u>it is the blood that maketh an atonement for the soul</u>. Leviticus 17:11*

- The priest whom God appointed would then take the blood of the sacrifice and present it to God for forgiveness of the sinner who confessed and brought the appropriate sacrifice.

Ten times it is stated in the ritual of the Old Testament sacrifices, that it is the priest who made atonement or a covering of sin with the blood of the sacrifice on behalf of sinners, (Leviticus 4:20, 4:26, 4:31, 4:35, 5:6, 5:10, 5:13, 5:16, 5:18, and 6:7).

- If God accepted the intercession of the priest on behalf of the sinner with the shed blood, the sinner's life was spared.

This process is discussed in detail in chapters four through six of the book of Leviticus.

How that Procedure Applies to Us Today

What God required in those rituals was a picture of what Jesus would have to do in order to provide for complete forgiveness of sins.

All Have Sinned

From the time man first became a sinner, man has sought for an acceptable offering whereby he could avoid the wages of sin in death, and earn eternal life by his own works. But no one, apart from Jesus, has overcome the grave. This is because we all have sinned.

For all have sinned, and <u>come short of</u> the glory of God. Romans 3:23

Jesus is God's Lamb for Eternal Salvation

The good news is that Jesus, God's Divine Son, left heaven for the purpose of providing a sacrifice in his own precious blood, whereby God could forgive sinners and give them eternal life.

The next day John [the Baptist] *seeth Jesus coming unto him, and saith, <u>Behold the Lamb of God</u>, which taketh away the sin of the world. John 1:29*

Forasmuch as ye know that ye were not redeemed with corruptible things, as silver and gold . . . But with the <u>precious blood of Christ, as of a Lamb without blemish and without spot</u>: Who verily was foreordained [by God] *before the foundation of the world* [or before man even sinned], *but was manifest in these last times for you, who by him do believe in God, that raised him up from the dead, and gave him glory; that your faith and hope might be in God. 1 Peter 1:18-21*

Jesus Died for the Sins of All Mankind

This was to prove God's love for the whole world.

For God so loved the world, that he gave his only only begotten Son, that whosoever believeth in him should not perish, but have everlasting life. For God sent not his Son into the world to condemn the world, but that the world through him might be saved. John 3:16-17

Jesus Rose Again and Ascended into Heaven with His Precious Blood

Just as the Levitical High Priest had to present the blood of the sacrifice when approaching God in the Most Holy Place of the Temple in Jerusalem, Jesus had to do the same in heaven for us.

But Christ being come an high priest of good things to come, by a greater and more perfect tabernacle, not made with hands, that is to say, not of this building [referring to the Temple in Jerusalem]*; Neither by the blood of goats and calves, but by his own blood he entered in once into the holy place* [in heaven]*, having obtained eternal redemption for us [or eternal forgiveness of sins]. Hebrews 9:11-12*

Jesus Now Serves as Our Great High Priest Before God in Heaven

We now have a great high priest in heaven (the Lord Jesus) who is eager to intercede before his Father in heaven on behalf of sinners.

Now of the things which we have spoken this is the sum: <u>We have such an high priest</u> [speaking of Jesus], *<u>who is set on the right hand of the throne of the Majesty in the heavens</u>* [referring to God the Father]. *Hebrews 8:1*

He does so as God's appointed Mediator to represent sinners before God and to reconcile man to God.

For there is one God [the Father] *and <u>one mediator between God and men</u>, <u>the man Christ Jesus</u>; Who gave himself a ransom for all 1 Timothy 2:5-6*

That is why Christ Jesus became a man; in order to represent the cause of sinful man before God. Also notice that the apostle Paul points out that Jesus paid the "ransom" price, or court costs for all, so that all could be saved.

<u>Jesus Only Intercedes For Sinners</u>
<u>Who Repent and Believe in Him</u>

Just as the Levitical Priests only interceded on behalf of the sinner who repented towards God whose Law he had transgressed, confessed his sin, and presented the acceptable blood sacrifice that God would accept; in the same way Jesus only intercedes for those sinners who repent towards God, confess that they are sinners, and come to God by him for their salvation.

Wherefore he [Jesus] *is able also to save them to the uttermost* [or completely] *<u>that come unto God by him</u>, seeing he ever liveth to make intercession for them. Hebrews 7:25*

Only by placing one's faith in the blood of Christ, is God just to forgive a sinner.

Whom [Jesus] *God hath set forth to be a propi-tiation* [to appease God's wrath] *through [the sinner's] <u>faith in his blood</u>* [Christ's blood], *to declare his* [God's] *righteousness for the remission* [or forgiveness] *of sins . . . that <u>he might be just, and the justifier of him which believeth in Jesus</u>. Romans 3:25-26*

<u>What Every Sinner Must Do To Be Saved</u>
<u>Repent and Believe the Gospel!</u>

This means that we truly regret having sinned against God, and are willing to tell Him so in prayer. Jesus said when he was on the earth that. . .

. . . except ye repent, ye shall all likewise perish. Luke 13:3

This also means that you are willing to do whatever God commands you to do to be saved, and that is to believe in the Lord Jesus Christ.

Testifying both to the Jews, and also to the Greeks, <u>repentance toward God</u> [the Father] *<u>and faith toward our Lord Jesus Christ</u>. Acts 20:21*

But as many as received him [the Lord Jesus], *to them gave he power to become the sons of God, <u>even to them that believe on his name</u>. John 1:12*

And they said, <u>Believe on the Lord Jesus Christ</u>, and thou shalt be saved . . Acts 16:31

This means that we totally reject any efforts of our own to save ourselves, but trust alone in the love and grace of

God, the goodness of Jesus Christ, and the value of his precious blood to save us eternally from the penalty of our sins.

> *For by grace* [or God's favor] *are ye saved through faith; and that* [being saved] *not of yourselves: it is the gift of God: Not of works, lest any man should boast. Ephesians 2:8-9*

Pray, Asking Jesus to Save You!

> *That if thou shalt confess with thy mouth* [calling out loud to God in prayer] *the Lord Jesus* [acknowledging him to be both God and man], *and shalt believe in thine heart that God hath raised him* [Jesus] *from the dead* [since we didn't see it with our eyes, and how could Jesus hear our prayers otherwise], *thou shalt be saved. Romans 10:9*

> *For whosoever shall call upon the name of the Lord* [Jesus] *shall be saved.*   *Romans 10:13*

Let me ask you, dear reader, a personal question. Have your ears ever heard you, with your own mouth, call upon the name of the Lord Jesus Christ; asking him to be your Lord and Savior, trusting alone in his goodness and not yours, and in his precious blood for your salvation?

It isn't the words you say, but how you say it. It requires that you first humble yourself before God and obey His command.

> *And the publican, standing afar of, would not lift up so much his eyes unto heaven, but smote upon his breast* [as a sign of sorrow for his sins], *saying, God be merciful to me a sinner. I* [Jesus] *tell you, this man went down to his house justified rather than the other* [a Pharisee, who only

boasted in his own goodness]*: for every one that exalteth himself shall be abased* [or brought low]*; and he that humbleth himself shall be exalted. Luke 18:13-14*

The Urgency of Our Response

If you have not obeyed the Gospel by meeting the above requirements for salvation, I urge you to do so right now while you still have time. I do so for four reasons:

First, you may not have the next hour to do so. Life is contingent upon every breath allowed by the grace of God.

> *And as it is appointed unto men once to die, but after this the judgment. Hebrews 9:27*

Second, Jesus could come to rapture those he has saved at any time (see chapter seven). If you have heard the truth of the Gospel, and rejected it because you love your sin and do not want God to change you, God will see to it that when you are left behind you are not given a second chance.

> *And then shall that Wicked* [the coming Anti-Christ] *be revealed, whom the Lord shall consume with the spirit of his mouth, and shall destroy with the brightness of his coming: Even him, whose coming is after the working of Satan with all power and signs and lying wonders, And with all deceivableness of unrighteousness in them that perish; because they received not the love of the truth, that they might be saved. And for this cause God shall send them strong delusion, that they should a lie, that they all might be damned who believed not the truth, but had pleasure in unrighteousness. 2 Thessalonians 2:8-12*

While many left behind in the Rapture will be saved during the Tribulation (cf. Revelation 6:9-11), not one of those Paul described as stated above will be saved. This is why the apostle Paul emphasized in his first epistle to the Corinthians that the time for them to respond to the Gospel is now.

> *(For he saith, I have heard thee in a time accept-ed, and in the day of salvation have I succoured thee: behold, now is the accepted time; behold, now is the day of salvation.) 2 Corinthians 6:2*

Third, God graciously leads the sinner to where he feels the need to repent towards God and be saved. But God can also then choose to harden the heart of the one who resists the goodness of God, so that he no longer feels the need to be saved. It is dangerous to play games with the convicting work of God in the heart.

> *Or despisest thou the riches of his goodness and forbearance and longsuffering; Not knowing that the goodness of God leadeth thee to repentance? But after thy hardness and impenitent heart trea-surest up unto thyself wrath against the day of wrath and revelation of the righteous judgment of God. . . Romans 2:4-5*

> *Therefore hath he mercy on whom he will have mercy, and whom he will he hardeneth. Romans 9:18*

Fourth, it will be Jesus who will condemn sinners for not believing in him for salvation.

This is because unbelieving sinners have rejected the plan God made in Christ before the foundation of the world for man's salvation. It is because they have not trusted in Christ to change them from their sinful condition. And it is because they cannot rightly accuse God of not loving them, for it is God's divine Son who died to save them who then condemns them.

> *For the Father judgeth no man, but hath <u>committed all judgment unto</u> the Son. John 5:22*

> *And I saw a great white throne, and him [Jesus] that sat on it, from whose face the earth and the heaven fled away; and there was found no place for them. And I saw the dead, small and great, stand before God; and the books were opened; and another book was opened, which is the book of life: and the dead were judged out of those things which were written in the books, according to their works . . .And <u>whosoever was not found written in the book of life</u> [having been saved beforehand by trusting in Jesus] <u>was cast into the lake of fire</u>. Revelation 20:11-15*

CONCLUSION

$\dagger$

In each chapter, I summarized essential truths involved in the Gospel of Jesus Christ. As I said in the Preface, just as key ingredients are specified for preparing a particular food, without which the meal being prepared would lack in taste and in quality, in the same way what is included in this book are key ingredients of the Christian Faith.

There is a reason Christianity is so named. The Christian Faith is based upon the person of the Lord Jesus Christ. No other one can save a sinner from his sins when he meets God in the day of judgment. Jesus said so!

> *Jesus saith unto him, <u>I am the way</u>, <u>the truth</u>, and <u>the life</u>: <u>no man</u> cometh unto the Father, <u>but by me</u>. John 14:6*

It is as simple as that.

> *<u>He that hath the Son hath life</u>; and <u>he that hath not</u> the Son of God <u>hath not life</u>. 1 John 5:12*

If you have called upon the name of the Lord Jesus Christ with sincerity of heart, you have life.

> *These things have I written unto you <u>that believe</u> on the name of the Son of God; <u>that ye may know</u>*

*that ye have eternal life, and that ye may believe
on the name of the Son of God. 1 John 5:13*

If you have not done so, please bow your head and do
so right now. Then make your confession of faith in Jesus
Christ public by going to a good local church and obeying
Christ's command to be publicly baptized.

*And Jesus came and spake unto them, saying, All
power is given unto me in heaven and in earth.
Go ye therefore, and teach all nations, baptizing
them in the name of the Father, and of the Son
[the Lord Jesus Christ] , and of the Holy Ghost
[or Holy Spirit]. Teaching them to observe all
things whatsoever I have commanded you: and,
lo, I am with you always, even unto the end of the
world. Amen. Matthew 28:18-20*

And what is a good local church? It is a church that, at
the very least, believes in the essential truths of the Gospel
as stated in this book. For apart from these essentials, the
Gospel of Jesus Christ would not be Good News!

If you have further questions, or would like for me to send
you some lessons on how to get started in your Christian life,
write me at Appalachian Bible College, 161 College Drive,
Mt. Hope WV 25880.

CPSIA information can be obtained at www.ICGtesting.com
Printed in the USA
BVOW021108240512

290972BV00001B/4/P

9 781619 969735